JUnit
Pocket Guide

JUnit
Pocket Guide

Kent Beck

Beijing · Cambridge · Farnham · Köln · Paris · Sebastopol · Taipei · Tokyo

JUnit Pocket Guide
by Kent Beck

Copyright © 2004 O'Reilly Media, Inc. All rights reserved.
Printed in the United States of America.

Published by O'Reilly Media, Inc., 1005 Gravenstein Highway North,
Sebastopol, CA 95472.

O'Reilly books may be purchased for educational, business, or sales
promotional use. Online editions are also available for most titles
(*safari.oreilly.com*). For more information, contact our corporate/
institutional sales department: (800) 998-9938 or *corporate@oreilly.com*.

Editor:	Mike Hendrickson
Production Editor:	Darren Kelly
Cover Designer:	Ellie Volckhausen
Interior Designer:	Melanie Wang

Printing History:

September 2004: First Edition.

0-596-00743-4
[C]

Contents

JUnit Pocket Guide

Automating Tests

Nearly every programmer tests his code. Testing with JUnit isn't a totally different activity from what you're doing right now. It's a different way of doing what you're already doing. The difference is between *testing*, that is checking that your program behaves as expected, and *having a battery of tests*, little programs that automatically check to ensure that your program behaves as expected. In this chapter we'll go from typical println( )-based testing code to a fully automated test.

Let's begin writing our first automated test. Imagine that we have been asked to test Java's built-in ArrayList. One bit of functionality to test is the method length ( ). When we create a new list it should have a length of 0. After we add an element the length should be 1. Imagine a little code snippet to test this:

```
List fixture= new ArrayList();
// fixture should be empty
Object element= new Object();
fixture.add(element);
// fixture should have one element
```

TIP

How do you pick good data values for tests? My habit is to pick a few representative values and to choose values that result in easy-to-check results. If I'm testing a currency converter, for example, an exchange rate of 2:1 is just as valuable as a programming tool as a "realistic" rate of 1.32471:1. For collections, like the one here, no elements and one element may be sufficient. Use induction to simplify testing. If "zero and one element work" implies "any number of elements work," use zero and one as your inputs.

A really simple way to check whether we are getting the results we expect is to print the size of the list before and after adding the element. If we get 0 and then 1, ArrayList is behaving as expected.

```
List fixture= new ArrayList();
System.out.println(fixture.size());
Object element= new Object();
fixture.add(element);
System.out.println(fixture.size());
```

Now, we would like to move from tests that require manual interpretation to tests that can run automatically. We can take one step by comparing the actual values and our expected values and just printing out booleans. Then, we can look at the printed output and make sure all the lines are true. If we ever see a false, we know something is wrong.

```
List fixture= new ArrayList();
System.out.println(fixture.size() == 0);
Object element= new Object();
fixture.add(element);
System.out.println(fixture.size() == 1);
```

Checking booleans is the kind of boring, tedious, error-prone, rote work that is easier for computers to handle than humans. Suppose we create a function that takes a boolean as its input and throws an exception only if the boolean is false.

```
void assertTrue(boolean condition) throws Exception {
    if (! condition)
        throw new Exception("Assertion failed");
}
```

Now our test output gets simpler. Nothing gets printed if the test succeeds. If we see an unhandled exception, we know something has gone wrong.

```
List fixture= new ArrayList();
assertTrue(fixture.size() == 0);
Object element= new Object();
fixture.add(element);
assertTrue(fixture.size() == 1);
```

This test is completely automated. Instead of just *testing* as we did with our first version, with this version we have an *automated test*.

We only have one test. When we go to write remove( ) we'll need another test. Then another for iterator( ). And another and another. We could write the infrastructure for all these tests from scratch. However, we would like to write the infrastructure once and then only need to write the unique parts of each test. JUnit is just such an infrastructure. Before diving into more details of writing tests, let's ask the question: why should developers write automated tests?

TIP

Installing JUnit

Download the latest junit.jar file from junit.org or use the one distributed with your IDE. Place it somewhere on your classpath. That should be all you need to do to begin using JUnit. If you have problems, go to www.junit.org.

Why Test?

This book shows you how to write automated tests using JUnit. JUnit is a framework that automates the tedious, repetitive parts of writing tests. JUnit:

- Runs tests automatically
- Runs many tests together and summarizes the results
- Provides a convenient place to collect the tests you've written
- Provides a convenient place for sharing the code used to create the objects you are going to test
- Compares actual results to expected results and reports differences

Having written similar test code ten times, Erich Gamma and I distilled what was common to all our test-writing activities into JUnit. It turns out that most of what goes on in writing tests is unique to each test, but there is sufficient commonality that there is leverage in creating a framework to capture the common elements.

Why should you, a programmer, automate tests? Isn't it enough that you have to design, analyze, architect, code, debug, build, and release your code? Why would you want to take on another job when there are people out there whose job it is to test?

While there are many rational explanations for why programmers should automate tests, for me the compelling argument is emotional. When I write automated tests I feel more confident in my work than when I don't write automated tests. From this confidence flows a host of benefits.

I like feeling confident. Without automated tests I often have a niggling sense that I have forgotten something. I'm afraid that my code, while it does everything I can think of at the moment, won't work in some case that I haven't yet thought of. Worse yet, I'm afraid that my code won't work in a case that I considered months ago but have now forgotten. When I run my tests I either get a green bar, which means everything so far is okay, or I get a red bar, which means one or more tests failed. If I have a failing test I know what to do—fix it.

Anxiety harms the rest of my professional activities. When I'm confident, I design better. I consider more radical alternatives that promise a small chance of dramatic improvement. When I'm feeling confident, I'm much more aware of other people—their moods, words, and ideas. I can be more responsive to my colleagues' needs. Communication improves, and the work flows more smoothly. When I'm confident, I don't feel rushed. When I'm not rushed, I'm much more likely to take the time to craft my code to gracefully handle a wider variety of inputs, not just the ones immediately in front of my face.

When I program *test-first* I can have confidence throughout the process. Tests give me confidence that I know what problem I'm trying to solve. I can write code that solves that problem. And I can be confident that the code works. It's as if the tests are a red carpet I roll out just in front of my feet. Justified confidence leads to good code, which leads to further justified confidence.

Time

There are two aspects of time and testing I want to cover here. The first is where the time comes from to write these automated tests. I am always looking for win-win-win programming practices, practices that provide:

- A win for me in the short term
- A win for me in the long term
- A win for my teammates and customers

The win for me in the long term comes from being able to change my code long after I've written it without accidentally breaking anything. Code that I can continue to change for a long time is code that I can charge for changing for a long time. The win for my teammates comes from the ease with which well-tested code can be integrated with the rest of the system. The win for my customers comes from the reduction in the number of defects in tested code and also from the option to continue adding features to tested code indefinitely.

Okay, that takes care of two of the wins. What is the short-term win in automating tests? If a programmer automating tests takes more time today than a programmer not automating tests today or even this week, then programmers won't automate tests. Where does the time come from today? In a word, debugging.

It wasn't until I had been automating tests for several years that I noticed that I didn't use the debugger. It wasn't that I used the debugger a little less. I only used the debugger every few months, and this from a programmer who used to live in the debugger. What was going on?

First, the tests act as a defect detector. Many times when I introduce a defect accidentally, a test immediately fails. When I say "immediately," I mean I know within seconds or minutes that I have broken something. When this happens, I often have several alternatives in mind, one of which I choose to implement. "Oh, just incrementing that doesn't work. I guess I'll have to recalculate." Instead of having to go into a debugger and figure out what went wrong, I can solve my problem a different way.

When I cause a problem in code I'm not working on directly, I still get immediate feedback about the problem. In this case, though, I won't necessarily have an alternative in mind. I do know, however, to stop right then and dig deeper into what is going on. The pattern of test failures gives me valuable clues into the problem, so often I don't have to resort to a debugger to find the problem. The tests themselves provide the tea leaves I can read to find the problem.

Which brings me to the second aspect of time I want to discuss with respect to automating tests: the Defect Cost Increase (DCI). DCI states that the sooner you test after the creation of an error, the greater your chance of finding the error and the less it costs to find and fix the error, as illustrated in Figure 1. This theory explains why leaving testing until just before releasing software is so expensive and error-prone. Most errors don't get caught at all. The cost of finding and then fixing the ones you do catch is so high that you have to play triage with the errors because you just can't afford to fix them all.

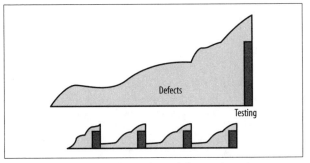

Figure 1. Frequent testing leaves fewer defects at the end

It is not possible to catch all the defects. However, testing more frequently reduces the number of defects left at the end. The value of fewer defects has to be traded off against the cost of testing. (This was always assumed to be a tradeoff.) If developers are more efficient writing automated tests, there is no tradeoff. Frequent testing doesn't cost; it pays.

Developers automating tests don't spend much time debugging. If you find an error in seconds or minutes and fix it, it is fixed. The time it takes is not significant enough to track or name. If it takes hours or days to track down a problem, fix it, and gain reasonable confidence that you haven't broken anything else, then we give that activity the name "debugging" (however long it takes).

When the person doing the testing and the person committing the errors are separate people, there is a natural limit to how close the testing can get to the introduction of the error.

This places a limit on the benefits you can gain from the DCI. By having the same person code and test, you can bring the proximity from days or weeks down to minutes. If the benefit gained from closer proximity is great enough, the programmer can visibly get more done even in a day, thus satisfying our need for the third, short-term, win.

"Perfect" is a Verb

The goal in most programming is not perfect code or perfect technique, but code and technique that are continually improving. One objection to programmers automating tests that I often hear is Dijkstra's saying that "Tests can prove the presence of defects but not their absence." While I would not presume to contradict Dijkstra, what he says is true but irrelevant. Most programmers make many mistakes. Automating tests is a way to make fewer mistakes. While your code will still not be perfect, even with excellent tests; you will likely see a dramatic reduction in defects once you start automating tests. And your effectiveness will continue to improve.

As testers have been telling us for years, there is a real art to testing effectively. The tests you write in your first month will be nowhere near as effective at catching defects as the tests you write after a year.

So, the goal of automating tests is justified confidence. You can use the confidence dividend to take more daring leaps in design, get along with your teammates better, improve relations with your customers, and go home every night with proof that the system is better now than it was this morning because of your efforts.

JUnit's Goals

Every framework has to resolve a set of constraints, some of which seem always to conflict with each other. JUnit is no exception; simultaneously tests should be:

- Easy to write. Test code should contain no extraneous overhead.

- Easy to learn to write. Because our target audience for JUnit is programmers who are not usually professional testers, we would like to minimize the barriers to test writing.

- Quick to execute. Tests should run fast so we can run them hundreds or thousands of times a day.

- Easy to execute. The tests should run at the touch of a button and present their results in a clear and unambiguous format.

- Isolated. Tests should not affect each other. If the order in which the tests are run changes, the results shouldn't change.

- Composable. We should be able to run any number or combination of tests together. This is a corollary of isolation.

There are two main clashes between these constraints:

- Easy to write versus easy to learn to write. Tests do not generally require all the flexibility of a programming language, especially not an object language. Many testing tools provide their own scripting language that only includes the minimum necessary features for writing tests. The resulting tests are easy to read and write because they have no noise distracting you from the content of the tests. However, learning yet another programming language and set of programming tools is inconvenient and clutters your mind.

- Isolated versus quick to execute. If you want the results of one test to have no effect on the results of another test, each test should create the full state of the world before it begins to execute and return the world to its original state when it finishes. However, setting up the world can take a long time: for example connecting to a database and initializing it to a known state using realistic data.

First, JUnit resolves these conflicts by using ordinary Java as the testing language. Sometimes the full power of Java is overkill for writing little straight-line tests, but by using Java we leverage all the experience and tools programmers already have in place. Since we are trying to convince reluctant testers, lowering the bar to writing those initial tests is particularly important. Second, JUnit errs on the side of isolation over quick execution. Isolated tests are valuable because they provide high-quality feedback. You don't get a report with a bunch of failed tests, which were really caused because one test at the beginning of the suite failed and left the world messed up for the rest of the tests. At the beginning, I was nervous about this bias towards isolation, but I also knew that there were many ways of solving performance problems. In practice, JUnit's orientation towards isolated tests encourages designs with a large number of simple objects. Each object can be tested quickly in isolation. The result is better designs *and* faster tests.

Another systematic bias in JUnit is that most tests succeed. When a test fails, that's a fact worth noting and reporting. The vast majority of tests should succeed and aren't worth commenting on except to count the number of tests that ran. This is an assumption that is really built into the reporting classes, not the core of JUnit. When the results of a test run are reported, you see how many tests were executed, but you only see details of those that failed.

JUnit is not a scripting language. Tests are expected to be fine grained, testing one aspect of one object. Hence, the first time a test fails, execution of that test halts, and JUnit reports the failure. There is an art to testing in many small tests, but thinking about fine-grained tests helps design.

While you test objects with JUnit, you do so only through those objects' public interface. Testing based only on publicly visible behavior encourages you to confront and solve difficult design problems earlier, before the results of poor design can infect large parts of the system.

Erich and I have always been explicit about our philosophy of JUnit and frameworks in general:

- Frameworks should be intersections not unions. We put into JUnit only those features required by all testing. Specialized needs can be met by extension projects.

- Do your best. We designed the core of JUnit, the `junit.framework` package described in the API section, to the best of our ability. Frameworks have widespread impact, good or bad, so they are worth lavish care.

- Evolve slowly. The current release, 3.8.1, has been out and stable for two years. We have vague plans for a 4.0 release, but without a compelling reason to add new functionality, we won't work on it. This gives all the people working on top of JUnit, various extenders and IDEs, confidence that their investment won't go to waste.

A good example of a feature we have left out of JUnit so far is automatically finding tests to run. This would be a useful feature if there were one universal way to implement it, but we haven't found one yet. Instead, we leave it to those writing test runners like those in Ant and the various IDEs to solve the test finding problem in ways that make sense for their tools. We have a simple mechanism, the static `suite( )`

method, that works reasonably well for those programming without an IDE.

Fixtures

One of the most time-consuming parts of writing tests is writing the code to set the world up in a known state and then return it to its original state when the test is complete. Here is a test of a server and client communicating:

```
public void testPing( ) {
    Server s= new Server( );
    s.start( );
    Client c= new Client( );
    c.start( );
    c.send("ping");
    assertEquals("ack", c.receive( ));
    c.stop( );
    s.stop( );
}
```

To implement this correctly, we have to wrap the stop( ) calls in a finally block so that if something goes wrong in sending or receiving, the client and server will still be stopped:

```
public void testPing( ) {
    Server s= new Server( );
    s.start( );
    try {
        Client c= new Client( );
        c.start( );
        try {
            c.send("ping");
            assertEquals("ack", c.receive( ));
        } finally {
            c.stop( );
        }
    } finally {
        s.stop( );
    }
}
```

The actual content of the test is lost in the noise of creating a predictable state of the world against which to test. And this example is much simpler than many of the situations you will encounter in real testing.

The problem gets even worse when you write several tests with a similar setup. Once we get "ping" working, we test to be sure that all the other messages gets the expected replies. Without some help from our testing framework we would have to duplicate the boilerplate for each test we write.

JUnit supports sharing the setup code. Before a test method is run, a template method called setUp( ) is invoked. setUp( ) is intended as the place where you create the objects against which you will test. Once the test runs, whether it succeeds or fails, another template method called tearDown( ) is invoked. setUp( ) and tearDown( ) will be called once for each test method run. While it might seem frugal to only run these methods once for all the test methods in a test-case class, this makes it hard to write tests that are completely independent of each other. Not only are setUp( ) and tearDown( ) run once for each test method, but the test methods are run in fresh instances of the test-case class.

I can refactor the test above using setUp( ) and tearDown( ) to concentrate the test on the stimulus and the expected response. First I declare the variables I am going to use as fields instead of method-local:

```
Server s;
Client c;
```

I put the object creation code in setUp( ):

```
protected void setUp( ) {
    s= new Server( );
    s.start( );
    c= new Client( );
    c.start( );
}
```

I put the code that restores the state of the world into tearDown( ). Notice that I use a finally clause so the server will stop even if the client fails to stop correctly.

```
protected void tearDown( ) {
    try {
        c.stop( );
    } finally {
        s.stop( );
    }
}
```

Finally I remove the redundant code from the test method:

```
public void testPing( ) {
    c.send("ping");
    assertEquals("ack", c.receive( ));
}
```

Now when I want to write another test with a client and server initialized in exactly the same way, I can just write the interesting part of the test:

```
public void testAdd( ) {
    c.send("add 2 2");
    assertEquals("4", c.receive( ));
}
```

The tests are now two lines that are easy to read instead of 14 deeply-nested lines.

More setUp( ) than tearDown( )

setUp( ) and tearDown( ) are nicely symmetrical in theory but not in practice. In practice, you only need to implement tearDown( ) if you have allocated external resources like files or sockets in setUp( ). If your setUp( ) just allocates plain Java objects, you can generally ignore tearDown( ). However, if you allocate many megabytes of objects, you might want to clear the variables pointing to those objects so they can be garbage-collected because the test case objects are not garbage-collected at any predictable time.

Variations

What happens when you have two tests with slightly different setups? There are two possibilities:

- If you put a little too much stuff into the setUp( ) method, move the variable part of the setUp( ) to the test method.
- You really have a different setUp( ), in which case you need a different test case class. Name the class after the difference in the setup.

Suite-Level Setup

JUnit doesn't provide convenient support for suite-level setup. There are a few good reasons to share fixtures between tests, but the vast majority of times I've seen shared fixtures, it was because there was an unresolved design problem.

For example, you might want to log in to a database once and then use that database connection in several tests. This makes your tests run faster. To do this, wrap the test suite returned by the static suite( ) method in a TestSetup, which overrides setUp( ) to open the database connection and tearDown( ) to close the connection.

```
class DatabaseTests extends TestSetup {
    DatabaseConnection connection;
    protected void setUp() throws Exception {
        connection= new DatabaseConnection("kent",
"password")
    }
    protected void tearDown() throws Exception {
        connection.close();
```

```
        }
    }
    public static Test suite() {
        Test suite= new TestSuite(this.class);
        return new DatabaseTests(suite);
    }
```

I can't emphasize enough that sharing fixtures between tests reduces the value of your tests. The underlying design problem is that objects are too closely bound together. You will have better results solving the design problem and then writing tests using stubs, rather than creating dependencies between tests at runtime and ignoring the opportunity to improve your design.

Testing Exceptions

How do you test exceptions? You can't directly assert that they are thrown. Instead you have to use Java's exception-handling facilities to write the test.

Suppose a factorial method should throw an IllegalArgumentException if it is passed a negative parameter. The test looks like this:

```
public void testNegative() {
    try {
        Factorial.compute(-1);
        fail();
    } catch (IllegalArgumentException expected) {
    }
}
```

If the call to compute( ) doesn't throw an exception, the subsequent call to fail( ) (a JUnit method) will halt the test and signal a problem with the test. If the expected exception is thrown, the catch block will be executed, and the test will continue executing.

Tests without Assertions

This test is a rare example of a valid test without any assertions. Usually when I see tests without assertions, it is because a programmer couldn't figure out how to get the test to pass and deleted the assertions instead of continuing to work. Sometimes the assertions are there but test some very generic condition, like checking to make sure an object is not null, instead of checking to make sure that precisely the expected object is calculated. Tests are your chance to say precisely what you mean in a particular case. The more precisely you specify your expectations, the more valuable the test.

Be precise when you declare what kind of exception you expect to be thrown. If you want a particular type of exception, be sure to say exactly what it is in the catch clause. If you expect certain information to be filled into the various fields of the exception, add assertions to check for that information. However, if you don't care what kind of exception gets thrown, just declare a generic Exception. I've found when doing this that some tests pass immediately. The naïve code for factorial, for example, will generate a StackOverflowError when passed a negative parameter. This might be good enough for your current purposes.

Another aspect of testing exceptions is what to do when a method you call declares an exception. Creating a FileWriter, for example, can throw an IOException. You can use a similar structure to the one above to catch the exception:

```
public void testWrite() {
    try {
        Writer w= new FileWriter("testing");
```

```
        } catch (IOException e) {
            fail();
        }
    }
```

If the IOException is thrown, the test will fail. There is a better way, however. If a test case throws an exception, JUnit records the test as having failed and saves the exception for later reporting. You can get the same results as the code above by writing:

```
public void testWrite() throws IOException {
    Writer w= new FileWriter("testing");
}
```

Because the test methods are invoked by reflection, the declaration of the exception doesn't have to propagate any further in your code. The simpler variant also gives you better feedback because JUnit reports the original exception with all of its information, instead of the generic JUnit exception thrown by the call to fail( ).

JUnit's Implementation

JUnit's implementation is a bit unusual, using techniques that are difficult to maintain in ordinary application code. Knowing a bit about the implementation can help as you write tests.

Consider a test case class with two test methods in it:

```
public class EmptyTest extends TestCase {
    List empty= new ArrayList();

    public void testSize() {
        assertEquals(0, empty.size());
    }

    public void testIsEmpty() {
        assertTrue(empty.isEmpty());
    }
}
```

When the test is run, the first thing JUnit does is convert the test class into a Test object: in this case a TestSuite containing two instances of EmptyTest, as shown in Figure 2:

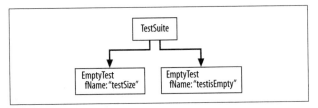

Figure 2. Tests about to be run

When the TestSuite is run, it runs each of the EmptyTests in turn. Each runs its own setUp( ) method, creating a fresh ArrayList for each test, as shown in Figure 3. This way, if one test modifies the list, the second test will not be affected.

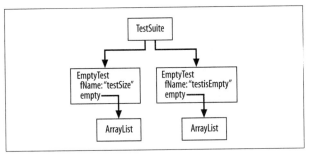

Figure 3. Tests after running, each with its own fixture

To run the test method itself, JUnit uses reflection to find the method named in fName and invokes it. I don't recommend this trick—called *Pluggable Selector* in the Smalltalk world—in application code because it makes it hard to statically analyze what code is called. You can't look at the code to decide whether a function is invoked, you have to look at the data values at runtime. However, using pluggable selectors in

JUnit makes writing the tests much simpler, so I think it's a reasonable tradeoff.

In short, one test-case class results in a two-level tree of objects when the tests are run. Each test method works with its own copy of the objects created by setUp( ). The result is tests that can run completely independently.

JUnit API

For most uses, JUnit has a simple API: subclass TestCase for your test cases and call assertTrue( ) or assertEquals( ) from time to time. However, for those of you who would like to look deeper into JUnit, here are all of its published methods and classes.

Overview

Most of the time you will encounter five classes or interfaces when you are using JUnit:

Assert
> A collection of static methods for checking actual values against expected values

Test
> The interface of all objects that act like tests

TestCase
> A single test

TestSuite
> A collection of tests

TestResult
> A summary of the results of running one or more tests

Figure 4 shows the relationship of the five basic classes in JUnit: Assert, Test, TestCase, TestSuite, and TestResult.

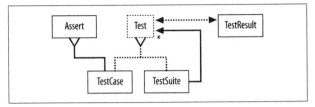

Figure 4. The five basic classes in JUnit

Assert

Most test cases written for JUnit are derived indirectly from the class Assert, which contains methods for automatically checking values and reporting discrepancies. The methods are declared static so you can write design-by-contract style assertions in your methods and have them reported through JUnit:

```
add(Object item) {
    junit.framework.Assert.assertNotNull(item);
    ...
```

Most of the time, though, you will be checking the assertions inside of tests.

There are two variants of each of the assertion methods: one takes as a parameter a message to be displayed with the error and one doesn't. The optional message is typically displayed when a failure is displayed. This can make debugging easier. Some people use the messages commonly; others (like me) don't. Here is the error message you get if you call assertTrue("Zero should equal zero", false):

```
1) testWithMessage(VectorTest)
junit.framework.AssertionFailedError: Zero should equal
zero
    at VectorTest.testWithMessage(VectorTest.java:7)
```

Table 1 shows all the varieties of assertions.

Table 1. Assertions

Assertion	Meaning
void assertTrue(boolean)	Reports an error if boolean is false.
void assertTrue(String, boolean)	Reports an error identified by String if boolean is false.
void assertFalse(boolean)	Reports an error if boolean is true.
void assertFalse(String, boolean)	Reports an error identified by String if boolean is true.
void assertNull(Object)	Reports an error if Object is not null.
void assertNull(String, Object)	Reports an error identified by String if Object is not null.
void assertNotNull(Object)	Reports an error if Object is null.
void assertNotNull(String, Object)	Reports an error identified by String if Object is null.
void assertSame(Object, Object)	Reports an error if the two Objects are not identical.
void assertSame(String, Object, Object)	Reports an error identified by String if the two Objects are not identical.
void assertNotSame(Object, Object)	Reports an error if the two Objects are identical.
void assertNotSame(String, Object, Object)	Reports an error identified by String if the two Objects are identical.
void assertEquals(Object, Object)	Reports an error if the two Objects are not equal (checked by calling equals( )).
void assertEquals(String, Object, Object)	Reports an error identified by String if the two Objects are not equal (checked by calling equals( )).
void assertEquals(String, String)	Reports an error if the two Strings are not equal. The error is reported as the delta between the two Strings.
void assertEquals(String, String, String)	Reports an error identified by String if the two Strings are not equal. The error is reported as the delta between the two Strings.

Table 1. Assertions (continued)

Assertion	Meaning
void assertEquals(boolean, boolean)	Reports an error if the two booleans are not equal.
void assertEquals(String, boolean, boolean)	Reports an error identified by String if the two booleans are not equal.
void assertEquals(byte, byte)	Reports an error if the two bytes are not equal.
void assertEquals(String, byte, byte)	Reports an error identified by String if the two bytes are not equal.
void assertEquals(char, char)	Reports an error if the two chars are not equal.
void assertEquals(String, char, char)	Reports an error identified by String if the two chars are not equal.
void assertEquals(short, short)	Reports an error if the two shorts are not equal.
void assertEquals(String, short, short)	Reports an error identified by String if the two shorts are not equal.
void assertEquals(int, int)	Reports an error if the two ints are not equal.
void assertEquals(String, int, int)	Reports an error identified by String if the two ints are not equal.
void assertEquals(long, long)	Reports an error if the two longs are not equal.
void assertEquals(String, long, long)	Reports an error identified by String if the two longs are not equal.
void assertEquals(float, float, float)	Reports an error if the first two floats are not within epsilon (the third float) of each other.
void assertEquals(String, float, float, float)	Reports an error identified by String if the first two floats are not within epsilon (the third float) of each other.
void assertEquals(double, double, double)	Reports an error if the first two doubles are not within epsilon (the third double) of each other.

Table 1. Assertions (continued)

Assertion	Meaning
void assertEquals(String, double, double, double)	Reports an error identified by String if the first two doubles are not within epsilon (the third double) of each other.

You may find that you need other assertions than these to compare objects specific to your project. Create your own Assert class to contain these assertions to simplify your tests.

Failing assertions all call a single bottleneck method, fail(String message), which throws an AssertionFailedError. There is also a variant which takes no parameters. Call fail( ) explicitly when your test encounters an error. The test for an expected exception is an example. Table 2 lists the bottleneck methods in JUnit.

Table 2. Bottleneck methods

Method	Action
void fail( )	Reports an error.
void fail(String)	Reports an error identified by String.

Test

Test is the generic interface implemented by all objects that can act as tests. It's a pity the interface is called Test, because implementors actually represent one or more tests. The two methods are shown in Table 3.

Table 3. Implementor Methods

Method	Meaning
int countTestCases( )	Return the number of tests.
void run(TestResult)	Run the tests and report the results on TestResult.

`TestCase` and `TestSuite` are the two most prominent implementors of `Test`. You can implement `Test` yourself. We deliberately kept it small so it would be easy to implement. For example, if you wanted to implement a test scripting language you could create a `TestScript` class and override the two methods in `Test`. `CountTestCases( )` would return 1. `run(TestResult)` would run a script with the results reported on the `TestResult`.

TestCase

Your test case classes will inherit from `junit.framework.TestCase`. Most of the time you will run tests from automatically created test suites. In this case each of your tests should be represented by a method named (by convention) `test*`.

`TestCase` implements `Test`. `CountTestCases( )` returns 1. `Run(TestResult)` runs `setUp( )`, runs the test method, and then runs `tearDown( )`, reporting any exceptions to the `TestResult`.

Table 4 shows the external protocol implemented by `TestCase`.

Table 4. Test case external protocols

Method	Meaning
`TestCase( )`	Primarily used for serialization. If you use it, be sure to call setName(String) immediately afterwards. We also use it internally so you don't have to override the constructor.
`TestCase(String)`	Creates a test case with the name String. Names are used to print the test case and often as the name of the test method to be run by reflection. Since Version 3.8.1 you don't need to override this constructor in your TestCase subclasses.
`String getName( )`	Return the name of the test case.
`void setName(String)`	Set the name of the test case to String.
`TestResult run( )`	Convenience method to run this test case and report it in TestResult.

Table 4. Test case external protocols (continued)

Method	Meaning
void runTest( )	Override with a testing method if you don't want the testing method to be invoked by reflection. Explicitly overriding runTest( ) is used in environments, like embedded Java, where you don't have access to reflection.

There are two template methods, setUp( ) and tearDown( ), you can override to create and dispose of the objects against which you are going to test. Table 5 shows these methods.

Table 5. Template methods

Method	Meaning
void setUp( )	Override to create objects against which to test. Each test that runs will be run in its own test case, and setUp( ) will be called separately for each one.
void tearDown( )	Override to dispose of objects no longer needed once the test has finished. In general, you only need to explicitly dispose of external resources (files or sockets, for example) in tearDown( ).

TestSuite

A TestSuite is a Composite of Tests. At its simplest, it contains a bunch of test cases, all of which are run when the suite is run. Since it is a Composite, however, a suite can contain suites which can contain suites and so on, making it easy to combine tests from various sources and run them together.

Generally, you will never see TestSuites directly. Most IDEs create suites for you. In case you have to create suites yourself, here is the public interface.

In addition to the Test protocol—run(TestResult) and countTestCases( )—TestSuite contains protocol to create named or unnamed instances. Table 6 shows the instance creation protocol for TestSuite.

Table 6. Creating named or un-named instances

Method	Meaning
TestSuite()	Return an empty TestSuite.
TestSuite(String)	Return an empty TestSuite named String.
TestSuite(Class)	Return a TestSuite containing an instance of Class for each method in the class named test*.
TestSuite(Class, String)	Return a TestSuite named String containing an instance of Class for each method in the class named test*.
String getName()	Return the name of the TestSuite.
void setName(String)	Set the name of the TestSuite to String.

TestSuite also contains protocol for adding and retrieving Tests, as shown in Table 7.

Table 7. Protocol for adding and retrieving Tests

Method	Meaning
void addTest(Test)	Add Test to the suite.
int testCount()	Return the number of Tests directly (not recursively) in this suite.
Enumeration tests()	Return the Tests directly in this suite.
Test testAt(int)	Return the Test at the index int.

TestResult

While you are running all these tests you need somewhere to store all the results: how many tests ran, which failed, and how long they took. TestResult collects results. A single TestResult is passed around the whole tree of tests. When a test runs or fails, the fact is noted in the TestResult. At the end of the run, the TestResult contains a summary of all the tests.

TestResult is also a subject that can be observed by other objects wanting to report testing progress. A graphical test runner might, for example, observe the TestResult and update a progress bar every time a test starts.

JUnit distinguishes between *failures* and *errors*. A failure is a violated JUnit assertion. An error is an unexpected exception. Sometimes this distinction proves useful since errors are generally easy to fix (e.g., NullPointerException means a variable wasn't initialized), while failures are generally harder to fix. If you have a big list of problems, it's best to tackle the errors first and see if you have any failures left when they are all fixed. Sometimes I wonder if this distinction is worth the trouble, though, as it complicates the interface. Table 8 summarizes the methods for reporting failures and errors.

Table 8. Distinguishing between failures and errors

Method	Meaning
void addError(Test, Throwable)	Record that running Test caused Throwable to be thrown unexpectedly.
void addFailure(Test, AssertionFailedError)	Record that running Test caused AssertionFailedError to be thrown unexpectedly.
Enumeration errors( )	Return the errors recorded.
Enumeration failures( )	Return the failures recorded.
int errorCount( )	Return the number of errors.
int failureCount( )	Return the number of failures.
int runCount( )	Return the total number of test cases run.
boolean wasSuccessful( )	Return whether or not all tests ran successfully.

(Enumeration is the old style of iterator. It remains in JUnit so we maintain compatibility with as many versions of Java as possible.)

If you want to register as an observer of a TestResult, you need to implement TestListener. To register, call addListener( ) as shown in Table 9

Table 9. TestListener and addListener

Method	Meaning
void addListener(TestListener)	Register TestListener to receive updates as results are recorded in the TestResult.

TestListeners implement the four methods shown in Table 10.

Table 10. TestListener callbacks

Method	Meaning
void startTest(Test)	Test is about to be run.
void endTest(Test)	Test has finished running.
void addError(Test, Throwable)	Test has thrown Throwable.
void addFailure(Test, AssertionFailedError)	Test has failed an assertion, throwing a kind of AssertionFailedError.

Package Structure

All the classes above come from junit.framework. Here are all the packages in JUnit:

junit.framework
    The basic classes in JUnit

runner
    Abstract support for running tests

swingui
    The Swing-based test runner

textui
    The text-based test runner

awtui
    The AWT-based test runner

extensions
    Experimental extensions to JUnit

Test-First Programming

You can use JUnit to write tests once you're done programming. Remember that we said that tests are more valuable the closer they are written in time to the time when an error might have been introduced. So instead of writing tests months after the code is "complete," we can write tests days or hours or minutes after the possible introduction of a defect. Why stop there? Why not write the tests a little before the possible introduction of a defect?

It turns out this is an old, old idea. Programmers used to look at an input tape and type in the output tape they expected to be produced by the input. Then they would program until they got the output they expected.

Test-first programming (part of test-driven development) takes this process and cranks it up to warp speed. With today's computational power, we have the opportunity to run thousands of tests thousands of times per day. We can use the feedback from all of these tests to program in small steps, each of which carries with it the assurance of a new automated test in addition to all the tests that have come before. The tests are like pitons, assuring you that, no matter what happens, once you've made progress you can only fall so far.

It felt strange to me at first, writing tests that I knew would fail. When you first write the test, it won't even compile because you are calling on objects and methods that haven't been defined yet. After a while, though, I began to get used to writing code that I knew wouldn't compile, and when it compiled, it wouldn't really run. When I was in school, I was always taught to think about interface and implementation separately. No one ever said how. Test-first programming is a pragmatic way to separate your thinking about implementation and interface. While you are writing the test you are thinking about interface—what does this object look like from the outside. When you go to make the test really work, you are thinking about pure implementation. The interface is fixed by the failing test.

What follows is necessarily an abbreviated introduction to test-first programming. You can explore the topic further in other books, like *Test Driven Development* (Addison-Wesley), by yours truly, or Dave Astels' excellent book *A Practical Guide to Test-Driven Development*.

Factorial Example

Here is a short example of programming a factorial function test-first. I always begin a test-first programming session with an outline of the tests I want to write. For factorial, I can only think of two important tests:

- 0
- More than 0

I always start with a simple example. My goal is never to have a failing test for more than a few seconds. That way I know exactly where I am. If I'm feeling adventuresome, or I'm just exploring, I might have a failing test for longer than that, but there is a useful discipline in being able to stay really close to your tests. The first test looks like this:

```
public void testOne() {
    assertEquals(1, factorial(1));
}
```

Notice that I've left the interface as simple as possible. In this case I don't need an interface any more complicated than a private method in the test-case class. I don't expect this interface to last, but leaving the interface simple for the moment allows me to gain experience with my code at the least possible cost, giving me as much information as possible to make better design choices later.

The implementation of factorial( ) can be simple since we only have the one test to satisfy so far:

```
private int factorial(int i) {
    return 1;
}
```

We run the test and it passes. Now we can write the second test. What input should we use? There is an art and science to correctly picking the domain of tests. Having read the books about testing, I rely on my gut to tell me how many inputs I need to test and which inputs I need to test. My tendency is to pick the simplest inputs that force me to write the code I think I need. Some people would pick a larger number, such as 5. For my purposes, it is just as good to pick 2, and it makes it easy for me to manually calculate the right answer (2). This introduces the risk that I pick simplistic inputs that don't really exercise the code, but I haven't found this to be a problem in practice. The attitude I take toward writing code is far more important than the precise test inputs I pick. If I set out to write solid code, I do, and even simple tests help me. If, for whatever reason, I'm not committed to solid code, no amount of ceremony around test writing is going to result in solid code. It's my attitude that needs adjusting. So for the sake of simplicity, my second test looks like this:

```
public void testTwo( ) {
    assertEquals(2, factorial(2));
}
```

Now I can write the recursive call to factorial:

```
private int factorial(int i) {
    if (1 == i) return 1;
    return i * factorial(i-1);
}
```

And the tests both pass. But what about inputs less than 1? I expect an exception to be thrown. Here's a test for that:

```
public void testZero( ) {
    try {
        factorial(0);
        fail( );
    } catch (IllegalArgumentException e) {
    }
}
```

This requires that we check the parameter before making the recursive call:

```
private int factorial(int i) {
    if (i < 1) throw new IllegalArgumentException( );
    if (1 == i) return 1;
    return i * factorial(i-1);
}
```

With these tests in place, we can confidently change the implementation of factorial, for example by replacing the recursive call with a loop. If we accidentally break the code, one of the tests should break.

Test-First Programming in Practice

Every program ever written has expected behavior in the face of expected inputs. Sometimes it can be a challenge to figure out how to measure the expected behavior, or to segregate the expected inputs into meaningful equivalence classes, but in the end it's always been possible for me, and it's always been valuable.

A recent challenge was figuring out how to write tests first for the code for *Contributing to Eclipse*. The example was a plug-in that extended the functionality of Eclipse. How do you test a plug-in that doesn't yet exist? It took us a couple of months of ordinary poke-and-peek exploratory testing before the lightbulb went on. First you make a test plug-in that depends on the plug-in you really want to create. This causes an error. To resolve the error, you have to create the real plug-in. Then you start writing tests in the test plug-in that expect the real plug-in to behave in certain ways that it doesn't, like displaying some information in a particular format.

Not all examples of test-first programming can be resolved this easily. One of the biggest challenges in all kinds of unit testing is figuring out how to deal with expensive, volatile external resources such as databases or servers. Whether you are writing tests before or after coding, *stubs* (the topic of the next section), will help you keep writing the valuable parts of tests and running these tests quickly and reliably.

Test-driven development (TDD) joins test-first programming and incremental design. In TDD you only add as much design as necessary to a system to pass the current tests with clean code. With test-first programming, you can take an upfront design and implement it, one test at a time. With TDD, you delay commitment to any particular design until the code calls for it. If you can get smooth enough at incremental design, this can lead to designs with no "fat," nothing put in oout of speculation or from fear.

Stubs

Tests that only test one thing are more informative than tests where failure can come from many sources. How can you isolate your tests from external influences? Simply put, replace the expensive, messy, unreliable, slow, complicated resources with stubs made from plain Java objects. For example, you can implement what is in reality a complicated computation by returning a constant, at least for the purposes of a single test.

A problem solved by stubs is the allocation of expensive external resources. If every test has to connect to a database, the tests are slow. If, instead, your design allows you to replace the real database with a stub database, you can write tests that are fast. With a bit more cleverness, you can create an option for running the tests with the real database or the stub database so you can use your tests for both local development or integration testing.

What is lost when stubbing? If the stub doesn't faithfully reproduce the behavior of the real object, you run the risk of having your tests pass but having the real system fail. Also, if you need the option to use a real or a stub object, you will have to pass the correct object to use as a parameter, often in a constructor, rather than rely on global variables. Overall, though, this results in a cleaner design.

Consider a program that has to send email. We could test it by actually sending email and then running an email client a few seconds later to fetch the email and check the message's contents. However, this is slow and prone to break unless every development machine has its email set up exactly the same way. Stubs provide an alternative.

```
public void testSending( ) {
    Transport t= new Transport( ) {
        public void send(Message m) {
            Address receiver= m.getAllRecipients[0];
            assertEquals("kentbeck@csi.com",
                receiver.toString( ));
            assertEquals("hello world\n",
                (String) m.getContent( ));
        }
    };
    MyObject o= new MyObject(t);
    o.run( );
}
```

In this test I have replaced the real Transport with a stub that doesn't actually send email, but rather checks the contents of the message that would have been sent had this not been a test. This test will run quickly and on any machine.

We should also test to make sure Transport works as expected. As long as these tests work, and the test above works, we can reasonably expect the whole system to work together.

Stubs and Good Design

One of the effects of using stubs is that your designs tend to improve. Widely used resources are accessed through a single façade so you can easily replace the resource with the stub. For example, instead of having direct database calls scattered throughout the code, you have a single Database object, an implementor of the IDatabase interface. Then you can create a stub implementation of IDatabase and install it before running your test. Functionality that needs to be stubbed at the same time tends to cluster in the same object, improving cohesion. By presenting the functionality with a single, coherent interface you reduce coupling with the rest of the system.

Self-Shunting

Sometimes you need to check that an object has been called correctly. You can create a full-blown stub of the object to be called, but then it can be inconvenient to check for correct results. A simpler solution is to use the test-case object itself as a stub, which is called self-shunting. The name is taken from the medical practice of installing a tube that takes blood from an artery and returns it to a vein to provide a convenient place for injecting drugs.

Here is an example. Suppose we want to test that the correct SQL query is generated when we ask a Librarian object to fetch us some accounts. First, we make our test case class an implementor of IDatabase:

```
public class QueryTest
    extends TestCase
    implements IDatabase
```

Next we implement the one IDatabase method, query( ), to check to make sure that the correct SQL is generated. We also set a flag so we can detect if the database is not called at all:

```
public boolean wasCalled= false;

public void query(String query) {
    assertEquals("select * from Accounts", query);
    wasCalled= true;
}
```

Now we can write our test. Notice that we create the Librarian with a particular database instead of relying on a single global database. This style of design is encouraged by stubbing. It reduces the coupling between objects and improves reuse.

```
public void testQuery( ) {
    Librarian l= new Librarian(this);
    l.fetchAccounts( );
    assertTrue(wasCalled);
}
```

The biggest problem with shunting is that if you are unfamiliar with the technique, the tests can be hard to read. What is going on here? Why is a test case also a database? Once you get used to the idiom, the tests are easy to read. Everything you need to understand the test is in one class. Another problem occurs when shunting interfaces with many methods. If there are three tests and 100 stubbed-out methods, few of which even have stubbed implementations, it can be hard to find the real tests amongst all that noise. The best solution to this problem is to not have interfaces with hundreds of methods. If you do have wide interfaces, you will have to choose between cluttering the test-case class with lots of trivial methods and the additional complexity of a separate class for the stub.

Testing listeners is another good use for shunting. Refer to `junit.tests.framework.TestListenerTest` for an example.

Other Uses for Tests

Once you get used to writing automated tests you will likely discover more uses for tests. Here are some of my favorites.

Debugging Tests

When I get a defect report, my impulse is to fix the defect as quickly as possible. This impulse has never served me well. I'm likely to cause another defect with my "fix."

With tests, I have a ritual I can use to hold my impulse in check.

1. I verify that I can reproduce the defect.
2. I find the smallest-scale demonstration of the defect in the code. For example, if a number appears incorrectly in a window, I find the object that is computing that number.

3. I write an automated test that fails but will succeed when the defect is fixed.

4. I fix the defect.

The search for the smallest reliable reproduction of the defect gives me a chance to really look at the cause of the defect. The test I write improves the chances that when I fix the defect, I really fix it (without tests, I have a tendency to cause a new defect when I fix a defect). All the other tests I have reduce the chances of inadvertently causing another problem. Because I add the test to the global test suite, I reduce the chances of accidentally undoing a fix—another persistent problem I've experienced.

I recommend finding a colleague and adopting the above ritual for fixing defects together. When you just can't think of a test for a defect, that's a good time to work on it with a partner. After a while, "thinking in tests" will become a habit. In the meantime, it's good to share the pain, frustration, eventual success, and satisfaction with a colleague.

Learning an API with Tests

Another way I use tests is when I need to learn a new API. If I use a new API to solve a new problem, I have two variables in play. I don't know whether problems are caused because my overall approach to solving the problem is wrong or whether it's my use of the API. Exercising the API with tests removes one of those variables.

For example, suppose I've just been handed a new set of collection classes. One, BoundedList, is only supposed to hold a fixed number of elements. An attempt to add too many elements should result in an exception. I think I understand this description, but do I really? Only experience will tell. How are you going to get that experience? Writing tests is a simple way that gives you immediate and concrete feedback.

What's my first test? I want to be sure the collection behaves like other collections, unless I add too many items. Here's what I write:

```
public void testOverflow( ) {
    List bounded= new BoundedList(1);
    Object element= new Object( );
    bounded.add(element);
    assertTrue(bounded.contains(element));
    try {
        bounded.add(element);
        fail("Should have thrown exception");
    } catch (CollectionOverflowException e) {
    }
}
```

I can go through the rest of the API, writing tests whenever I hit a method I want to make sure I understand. When I'm trying to learn a new API and use it for real at the same time, my mind is divided between the two tasks. Writing tests to learn an API goes more quickly, because I'm concentrating on learning. With the learning firmly in place, I can go ahead and solve my real problem with confidence.

Documenting Assumptions with Tests

Suppose you decide to use an external package as part of your development. You are now exposed to the risks that the package won't behave as you expect and that future versions of the package will change in subtle ways that will break your code without you knowing it. How can you inexpensively address these risks?

One way is to write a test every time you make an assumption about how the package works. If you test passes, your assumption is valid.

Suppose I am writing a test runner that is going to use the automatic test suite creation built into JUnit. I assume that if I have a test-case class with one test in it and I create a suite for that class, the suite returned should have a single test in it. I can say this with a test:

```
public class ExampleSuite extends TestCase {
    public void testNothing() {
    }
}
public void testSuiteBuilding() {
    TestSuite suite= new TestSuite(ExampleSuite.class);
    assertEquals(1, suite.countTestCases());
}
```

If I have the discipline to document all of my assumptions with tests, then future releases of packages hold no fear for me. The first thing I do is run my assumption suite. If it passes, I expect my system to continue working. If it doesn't, I need to track down what has changed because it is pretty much guaranteed that my system won't work any more.

Cross-Team Tests

When you document assumptions with tests, you own the tests. This assumes an arms-length relationship between you and the supplier of the package on which you are building. If you want or have a closer relationship with a supplier, you can use the tests as a way of coordinating your activities.

When you want to agree on an API with a supplier, you can jointly write and maintain the tests. Sit down together and code the tests so you reveal as many assumptions as possible. Hidden assumptions are the death of cooperation. The tests tell the supplier exactly what is expected of them. They should come back when the tests all run. If it is impossible to get a test to run as written, then it's time to renegotiate the API. If no one changes the tests unilaterally, the chances of smooth integration go way up.

By adding stubs to tests, you can further decouple two teams. If you not only write the tests but also get them to run with stub objects too, two teams can develop independently. The supplier team's job is to make the tests run by replacing the stub objects with real implementations. The customer's job is to make their own code work with the stub objects until such time as they have the real implementation.

For example, suppose I want a simple little XML parser from you. Together we write this test:

```
public void testParsing( ) {
    IXMLParser parser= new StubXMLParser( );
    INode tree= parser.
        parse("<parent><child/></parent>");
    assertEquals("parent", tree.getName( ));
    assertEquals("child",
        tree.getChild(0).getName( ));
}
```

There are two interfaces in the API, IXMLParser and INode. We can provide trivial implementations of them, enough so I can begin coding as if parsing really works. The parser just returns a hardwired node:

```
public class StubXMLParser implements IXMLParser {
    public INode parse(String source) {
        return new Node("parent");
    }
}
```

The INode implementation is more complete, but it still returns a hardwired subnode:

```
class StubNode implements INode {
    protected String name;

    public StubNode(String name) {
        this.name= name;
    }

    public String getName( ) {
        return name;
    }

    public INode getChild(int index) {
        return new StubNode("child");
    }
}
```

I talked to a team who used this approach of combining tests with stub implementations. Their supplier was a hardware team creating customer chips. When a new version of the chip arrived, the first thing they did was run the tests. If the tests didn't run, it wasn't worth the cost of testing any of the rest of the system, because the tests documented the assumptions the software made about the hardware. With the stub implementation, though, the software team could begin developing as if the hardware was already complete (subject to the usual discovery of deeply buried assumptions when the real hardware became available).

Story of JUnit

Tests and testing were kind of unmentionable topics when I went to programmer school. If you were a good programmer, when you got out you'd get to program. If you weren't so good, you'd have to be a tester. I went from there to the Smalltalk world, where we tried to maintain a Zen-like oneness with our code so we could intuit if there was some kind of problem with our programs. I didn't writte any repeatable, automated tests.

After I'd been in the work world for about eight years, I had the opportunity to work with a wizard compiler writer, Christopher Glaeser. Christopher wrote five lines of test code for every line of compiler he wrote, and his tests were all completely automated. Every night he'd kick off his suite of tests. In the morning he'd know whether what he'd done the day before was working or not and whether he'd accidentally caused himself any problems. I was amazed at his productivity and quality, as well as his calm demeanor in a crazy environment. The tests gave him a kind of emotional certainty that I really wished I had.

When I started consulting, I remembered this experience. For years I had played with ways of writing and running automated tests, but I was not satisfied. One day I was about to leave for a consulting assignment, and I knew I wanted to advise them to write tests. It wouldn't be sporting to tell them to write tests but not tell them how. I sat down with Smalltalk and wrote a tiny framework—three classes and 12 methods. When the framework was small, it made it possible to write tests and run them. There wasn't even a user interface. You ran the tests, and the results printed on a console.

My client took the framework and started using it immediately. I wasn't sure that I had anything valuable, though, because the framework was so simple. I gave it to Hal Hildebrand, one of the smartest programmers I know. One week later, I didn't hear anything. One month later, I didn't hear anything. "Ah well," I thought, "just as I suspected. There's nothing there."

Then I got a really remarkable message. Hal had some tough bugs that he hadn't been able to track down. After a month of fruitless effort, he decided to give up and use this little framework to write tests for all of his lowest-level data structures, even though he was absolutely sure they all worked. You can probably guess the rest of the story. He found a bunch of defects in the simple little objects sitting beneath the whole system. Once he fixed those defects, the whole system began running perfectly.

I had confirmation that the framework was valuable, even for difficult problems. I started distributing it free inside the Smalltalk community.

That was in 1994. In 1997, while living in Zurich with my family, I caught up with Erich Gamma, a friend I met working on software patterns. He kept trying to convince me to learn Java, but I resisted because I liked Smalltalk so much. However, it became clear that Java was going to be important.

We happened to be flying together going to Atlanta to OOP-SLA, the big object-oriented programming conference. I wanted to learn Java. He wanted to see this framework I'd been talking about. What could be more natural to a couple of geeks in cramped quarters than to pull out a laptop and start coding?

Three hours later, we had the basics of JUnit done, and I had learned the basics of Java. We were careful to write tests for all of our testing infrastructure and, in a case of gratuitous complexity, even to write them first. This was a bit of a trick when we didn't have a framework to begin with. Once again, the resulting framework was so simple that we were a little embarrassed to show it to anyone else. Martin Fowler was our guinea pig this time. By the time the conference was over, he had already started to distribute the framework to friends.

Once Erich and I were back in Zurich, we started talking about what to call this little framework. JUnit captured our intention for the framework, which was to help programmers test individual objects. Around the same time, André Weinand wrote the AWT-based user interface, and we were ready for our first public release.

The biggest evolution of the framework classes was extracting the `Assert` class. `TestCase` was the only class. Then we noticed that there were all these `assert*` methods that had nothing to do with the methods for running a test, like `setUp( )` and `tearDown( )`. So we extracted a superclass and pushed up all the methods we could. They were still instance methods. Then Erich noticed that we could change the methods to static because none of them relied on any instance state. We could make them static without breaking already-written tests because statics are inherited. Doing so would make it possible for design-by-contract-style assertions to live alongside JUnit assertions.

Some commentators have complained about this relationship between `TestCase` and `Assert`. Since programmer convenience is one of the goals of JUnit, I'm perfectly content that `TestCase` inherits from `Assert`, because it makes tests less noisy, more communicative, and easier to write. It is an unusual use of inheritance, but inheritance is just a tool to help us realize our goals, not an abstract philosophical mechanism. I would rather write:

```
assertTrue(flag);
```

than:

```
Assert.assertTrue(flag);
```

Other people have extended JUnit in various ways, described in the section "Extending JUnit." There are also ports to, at last count, 28 other languages. This points out that the problems solved by JUnit are universal, as are the basic elements of the solutions.

There is a social aspect to the adoption of JUnit. Ten years ago, if you asked expert programmers whether they wrote automated tests, you would get almost unanimous "no"s. Programmers wrote programs. Testers wrote tests. JUnit appeared just as cracks began to appear in this strict division of labor. JUnit also fed this trend by providing an easily understood tool that leveraged all of a programmer's existing skills, lowering the barrier to begin writing tests.

JUnit by itself solves a single, cohesive problem. Further progress can come at the periphery by adding better test runners, integrating more tightly with IDEs, and adding tools that amplify the effectiveness of existing tests. Erich and I enjoy thinking of ways to further clarify and simplify the core of JUnit.

Extending JUnit

You can extend JUnit in many different ways to make writing tests easier and improve the feedback you get from running tests. Here are common ways of refining JUnit for your particular uses.

Subclass TestCase

Gather utility methods in an abstract subclass of TestCase and derive your test case classes from that class. This is one of the simplest ways to extend JUnit.

Assert *classes*

Create your own classes containing special-purpose assertions. One common extension is an assertion that compares arrays, but you can also compare other types of objects.

TestDecorator

> You can wrap test cases or test suites in a subclass of TestDecorator to perform some action before and after the test runs.

Implement Test

> The Test interface is narrow and easy to implement. You can implement a Test that runs data-driven tests, such as tests for various data files in a directory.

Subclass TestResult

> By passing a special-purpose TestResult to the run( ) method, you can collect extra information about the tests that run. I implemented a simple coverage tester, for example, using a subclass of TestResult.

Implement TestListener

> You don't necessarily have to write a whole subclass of TestResult. You can also implement a new TestListener and attach it to the TestResult before running the tests.

New Test Runner

> Write your own test runner, interactive or not, if you need different feedback from the execution of tests.

Extensions

We have tried to keep JUnit as simple as possible, to accommodate as many different styles of usage as possible. There are many useful extensions that others have created for more specialized purposes. Here are a few you may want to try:

> JUnitPerf
> HttpUnit
> JWebUnit
> Cactus
> JFCUnit
> JXUnit
> Jester

JUnit and Ant

Ant, the open source automated build tool, comes with a task to run JUnit tests, report results, and optionally stop the build if a test fails. This chapter introduces the options available in the JUnit task and how they might be used. The JUnit task includes many more options than I cover here. These are intended to get your started.

The JUnit task is an optional task. To enable Ant to find it, make sure you have the file *optional.jar* placed somewhere on the classpath. One place Ant is sure to find it is *ANT_HOME/lib*. Ant also needs access to the JUnit files. Placing *junit.jar* in *ANT_HOME/lib* makes JUnit accessible if it is not accessible elsewhere in the classpath.

Here is a simple Ant build file that just runs tests in a Java class called guide.SampleTest:

```
<project name="pocket guide" default="test">
    <target name="test">
        <junit>
            <test name="guide.SampleTest"/>
        </junit>
    </target>
</project>
```

By default there is no output from successful tests:

```
Buildfile: ...\build.xml
test:
BUILD SUCCESSFUL
```

If we put a call to fail( ) in SampleTest, we get feedback that the test failed:

```
Buildfile: ...\build.xml
test:
    [junit] TEST guide.SampleTest FAILED
BUILD SUCCESSFUL
```

Notice that the build was still considered successful even though a test failed. This betrays an interesting bias on the part of the writer of the JUnit task. I prefer to assume that if a

---

test doesn't work, the system doesn't work. The haltonfailure property causes the build to fail if a test fails:

```
<junit haltonfailure="on">
    <test name="guide.SampleTest"/>
</junit>
```

Now when the test fails, the build fails too:

```
Buildfile: ...\build.xml
test:
BUILD FAILED: ...\build.xml:3: Test guide.SampleTest
failed
```

If you watch the Ant output to track build progress, you can have the JUnit task write a one line summary when a test starts and completes by setting the printsummary attribute:

```
<junit printsummary="on">
    <test name="guide.SampleTest"/>
</junit>
```

Now a line is printed for each test as well as a line summarizing the results for all tests run by this task:

```
Buildfile: ...\build.xml
test:
    [junit] Running guide.SampleTest
    [junit] Tests run: 1, Failures: 1, Errors: 0, Time
elapsed: 0 sec
    [junit] TEST guide.SampleTest FAILED
BUILD SUCCESSFUL
```

I sometimes print debugging information in tests if I can't figure out how to just write another test. (If I take the time, I always find a way to write another test.) The JUnit task offers the showoutput attribute to print such information with the other task output:

```
<junit showoutput="true">
    <test name="guide.SampleTest"/>
</junit>
```

If I write a message to System.out inside my test case, it now appears in the Ant output:

```
Buildfile: ...\build.xml
test:
```

```
    [junit] Here is some output from a test
BUILD SUCCESSFUL
```

More About Running Tests

So far we've seen only the most basic way to run tests using the test element. The test element also gives you the opportunity to override the values of `haltonfailure` and `haltonerror` for a given test.

The batchtest element creates and runs a test element for each file in a file set. With two test classes, `SampleTest` and `AnotherTest`, the following batchtest runs them both:

```
<junit>
    <formatter type="brief" usefile="false"/>
    <batchtest>
        <fileset dir=".">
            <include name="**/*Test.java"/>
        </fileset>
    </batchtest>
</junit>
```

The output is just as if each test class had been declared in its own test element.

```
Buildfile: ...\build.xml
test:
    [junit] Testsuite: guide.AnotherTest
    [junit] Tests run: 1, Failures: 0, Errors: 0, Time
elapsed: 0 sec
    [junit] Testsuite: guide.SampleTest
    [junit] Tests run: 1, Failures: 0, Errors: 0, Time
elapsed: 0 sec
BUILD SUCCESSFUL
```

Formatting Feedback

The JUnit task includes a nested element describing a formatter for printing or otherwise processing feedback from tests. There are three built-in formatters, or you can write your own. The simplest formatter is called `brief`, and it is invoked with the type attribute of the `formatter` element like this:

```
<junit>
    <formatter type="brief" usefile="false"/>
    <test name="guide.SampleTest"/>
</junit>
```

I have set the usefile attribute to false so the formatter writes output to the console. The results look just like the results of setting the printsummary attribute to on:

```
Buildfile: ...\build.xml
test:
    [junit] Testsuite: guide.SampleTest
    [junit] Tests run: 1, Failures: 0, Errors: 0, Time
elapsed: 0 sec
BUILD SUCCESSFUL
```

If I insert a call to fail( ) in my test case, the formatter prints out a stack trace of where the error occurred:

```
Buildfile: ...\build.xml
test:
    [junit] Testsuite: guide.SampleTest
    [junit] Tests run: 1, Failures: 1, Errors: 0, Time
elapsed: 0 sec
    [junit] Testcase: testEmpty(guide.SampleTest):FAILED
    [junit] null
    [junit] junit.framework.AssertionFailedError
    [junit] at guide.SampleTest.testEmpty(SampleTest.java:
8)
    ...
    [junit] TEST guide.SampleTest FAILED
BUILD SUCCESSFUL
```

The plain formatter prints out how long each test case took to run:

```
<junit>
    <formatter type="plain" usefile="false"/>
    <test name="guide.SampleTest"/>
</junit>
Buildfile: ...\build.xml
test:
    [junit] Testsuite: guide.SampleTest
    [junit] Tests run: 1, Failures: 0, Errors: 0, Time
elapsed: 0 sec
    [junit] Testcase: testEmpty took 0 sec
BUILD SUCCESSFUL
```

The XML formatter writes the same information, but in a format suitable for post processing. Set the type attribute to xml to obtain it. Notice that I've eliminated the usefile attribute. By default, the output goes to a file whose name is derived from the name of the class called for in the test element.

```
<junit>
    <formatter type="xml"/>
    <test name="guide.SampleTest"/>
</junit>
```

Here is the output for a test that fails:

```
<testsuite name="guide.SampleTest" tests="1" failures="1"
errors="0" time="0.02">
  <properties>
    ...
  </properties>
  <testcase name="testEmpty" classname="guide.SampleTest"
time="0.0">
    <failure type="junit.framework.AssertionFailedError">
    junit.framework.AssertionFailedError
    at guide.SampleTest.testEmpty(SampleTest.java:8)
    ...
    </failure>
  </testcase>
</testsuite>
```

You are not limited to the built-in formatters. You can write your own by creating a class that implements the interface org.apache.tools.ant.taskdefs.optional.junit. JUnitResultFormatter. Here is a simple formatter that beeps whenever a test fails:

```
public class BeepFormatter
    implements JUnitResultFormatter {
    public void addFailure(
        Test test, AssertionFailedError t) {
            Toolkit.getDefaultToolkit().beep();
    }
    ...// stub implementations of other methods
}
```

Invoke this formatter with the classname attribute of the formatter element:

```
<junit>
    <formatter classname="guide.BeepFormatter"/>
    <test name="guide.SampleTest"/>
</junit>
```

You can declare as many formatters as you want in the build file.

Conclusion

By integrating JUnit tests with Ant, you can have the advantages of automatically building an entire system with the advantages of fine-grained feedback from automated tests. The result is more confidence in the system being built and quicker identification of errors.

Running JUnit Standalone

JUnit comes with three user interfaces:

- Text
- AWT
- Swing

Text

The text user interface gives you a command-line interface for running tests and textual feedback about test progress and results. Invoke the text test runner this way:

```
java junit.textui.TestRunner [-wait] TestClassName
```

The –wait option doesn't terminate the test runner until a character has been typed at the console. This is useful if you are running the tests in a window that stays open only as long as the test runner is active.

Here are the results of running JUnit's own tests. The periods represent the start of a new test case. "F" or "E" represent a failure or error. After all the tests are run, the stack traces of all failures and errors are printed followed by a summary of the number of tests run and the number of failures and errors.

```
.........................................
..............................F........
.........
Time: 1.061
There was 1 failure:
1) testJarClassLoading(junit.tests.runner.
TestCaseClassLoaderTest)junit.framework.
AssertionFailedError: Cannot find test.jar
    at junit.tests.runner.TestCaseClassLoaderTest.
testJarClassLoading(TestCaseClassLoaderTest.java:31)
    at sun.reflect.NativeMethodAccessorImpl.invoke0(Native
Method)
    at sun.reflect.NativeMethodAccessorImpl.
invoke(NativeMethodAccessorImpl.java:39)
    at sun.reflect.DelegatingMethodAccessorImpl.
invoke(DelegatingMethodAccessorImpl.java:25)

FAILURES!!!
Tests run: 91,  Failures: 1,  Errors: 0
```

The output of the text test runner is ugly, but it is still useful from time to time. Its best feature is that it starts up very quickly. If you want to run tests every ten seconds, opening a window is too slow.

AWT

Figure 5 shows the AWT runner, the first graphical JUnit runner. Its primary advantage is that it is extremely simple. The original implementation was by André Weinand, with logo design by Erich Gamma and me.

The top Run button runs all the tests found in the class named in the fill-in field at the top. Errors and failures are listed below. The bottom Run button reruns the selected failing test case, with the results printed in the status bar at the bottom of the window.

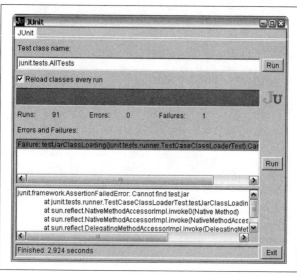

Figure 5. AWT-based Test Runner

The checkbox Reload classes every run deserves some explanation. It is inconvenient to have to open a new window every time you want to run tests. When you check "Reload," JUnit uses a custom class loader to throw away all of the test and model classes every time Run is pressed. This has the effect, under the right circumstances, of letting you leave the test runner window up. When you recompile, you need only press Run to get updated results.

I say "under the right circumstances" because this feature is the source of many problems. Some Java code expects to be using its own class loader and won't work when used with JUnit's loader. The short-term solution is to put a pattern that identifies classes relying on their own class loader into the *excluded.properties* file. The default *excluded.properties* file contains the following entries:

```
excluded.0=sun.*
excluded.1=com.sun.*
```

```
excluded.2=org.omg.*
excluded.3=javax.*
excluded.4=sunw.*
excluded.5=java.*
excluded.6=org.w3c.dom.*
excluded.7=org.xml.sax.*
excluded.8=net.jini.*
```

Any class matching one of these patterns will be loaded by its original class loader, not JUnit's. You don't want to put any classes on this list that will be recompiled between test runs, or you'll run your tests with obsolete classes and get inconsistent results.

The real solution to this problem is to start up a new JVM every time Run is pressed, so you are guaranteed to get the latest class files loaded. This feature is scheduled for JUnit 3.9. In the meantime, you need to be aware of class-loader-sensitive code and be sure to put those classes on the excluded list.

Swing

Figure 6, the Swing runner, is a transliteration of the AWT UI to use Swing widgets.

The top and bottom Run buttons in the Swing runner operate just like the same buttons in the AWT runner, rerunning all tests or a single test, respectively. The Swing runner also remembers the last several tests run. You can load one of these with the ... button.

The Results section shows a list of failures and errors and also a hierarchical view of your entire test suite, as shown in Figure 7.

The Test Hierarchy tab allows you to see all of your tests in context. Failed tests are highlighted with a red X.

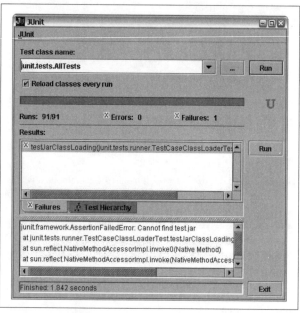

Figure 6. Swing-based Test Runner

JUnit and IDEs

All of the major Java IDEs directly support running JUnit tests and, to some degree, writing JUnit tests. My need for a JUnit/IDE integration is to be able to move between writing tests, writing code, running tests, and responding to failed tests as efficiently as possible. Here is a short summary of some IDEs with JUnit support and how I use them.

Eclipse

The JUnit support in Eclipse was written by Erich Gamma and co-op students. Eclipse works to make test writing and test running natural parts of the programming experience.

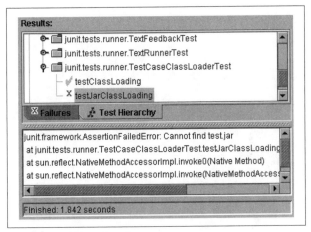

Figure 7. Test Hierarchy tab

Setting up a project so you can write tests

To write JUnit tests in an Eclipse project, you must first make JUnit visible. When you create a project, the second page of the project wizard gives you the option to change the build settings. Click the Libraries tab and press Add External JARs to add the JUnit JAR files to the project's build path. In the file browser navigate to your Eclipse installation directory, then to *plugins/org.junit*. Select *junit.jar*, as shown in Figure 8.

To add a test to an existing project, you can make JUnit visible from the Project Properties page. Select the Java Build Path page, the Libraries tab, and use Add External JARs to add *junit.jar* as above.

In Eclipse 3.0 this is even simpler. If you add a test case using the test case wizard, the wizard will offer to add the junit. jar for you.

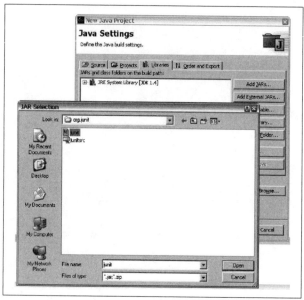

Figure 8. Project wizard change options

Writing tests

To create a test-case class, use subclass `junit.framework.TestCase`. You can use the test-case wizard (Figure 9) to fill in the superclass for you, as shown in Figure 10.

There is an editor template for writing a new test method. To invoke it, type test in a Java editor and press Ctrl-Space. Select test and you'll have a blank test method with the name of the method selected (see Figure 11).

Eclipse's Quick Fix facility saves a lot of work when used in conjunction with JUnit and TDD. You can write tests that refer to classes, methods, and members that don't exist yet, then use Quick Fix to create stubs for the missing elements with a minimum of fuss. Here I've written a test that calls `Factorial.calculate( )`, a nonexistent method on a nonex-

---

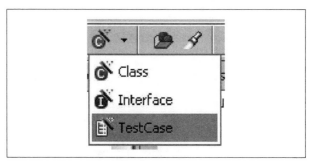

Figure 9. Invoking the TestCase Wizard

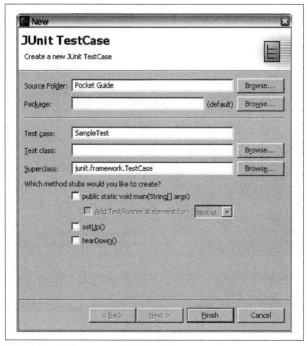

Figure 10. Creating a new TestCase

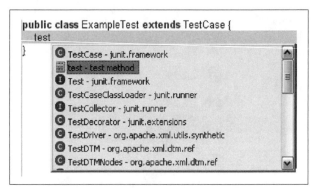

Figure 11. Creating a new Test Method

istent class. Clicking the light bulb in the left margin brings up a menu that contains exactly the activity we wish: to create a class (see Figure 12).

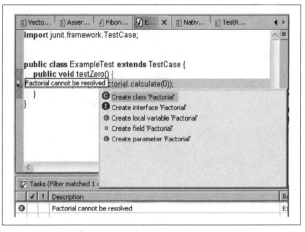

Figure 12. Creating a class with QuickFix

It takes only a few clicks to resolve the compile error, leaving us with a failing test ready to be satisfied.

Running tests

To run tests, select a project, package, class, or test method in the Package Explorer or Outline and choose Run → Run As → JUnit Test. The JUnit view will appear, showing you the results (see Figure 13).

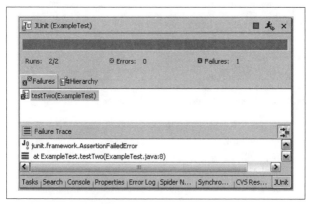

Figure 13. JUnit view with results

Double-clicking a failing test opens the definition of that test in the Java editor. Double-clicking a stack frame in the failure trace navigates to that line in the Java editor.

The Hierarchy tab in the JUnit view shows you all the tests run along with their status (pass, fail, or error). Double clicking one of the tests shows you the source for that test in the Java source code editor.

My setup when programming in Eclipse is to dock the JUnit view (drag it to the fast view bar) and set the JUnit preference to show only the view on failures or errors. The JUnit view icon fills up to indicate the progress being made, so I can go on with other tasks while the tests run. I am interrupted with the details only if an error occurs (as shown in Figure 14).

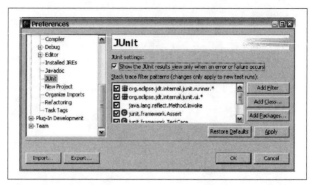

Figure 14. JUnit preferences: view only on error

Then I use ctrl-F11 to rerun the same tests after each programming change.

Extensions

Eclipse is built entirely from plug-ins with well-defined interfaces. You can implement these interfaces yourself to extend Eclipse to suit your own purposes. The JUnit support in Eclipse is also built as a plug-in. By implementing org. eclipse.jdt.junit.ITestRunListener, you view, log, or otherwise extend the running of tests. See org.eclipse.jdt. junit itself for details about writing your own Eclipse test runners.

JBuilder

JBuilder, from Borland, includes support for writing and running JUnit tests, as well as extensions to JUnit to help create reusable test fixtures.

Setting up a project so you can write tests

To write JUnit tests in JBuilder, you must first make JUnit visible inside the project. On the second page of the project creation wizard, select the Required Libraries tab and press

Add.... From there you can add JBuilder/JUnit (see Figure 15).

Figure 15. Adding the JUnit Library to a new project

For an existing project, you can edit the project properties to add JUnit to the Required Libraries, as shown in Figure 16.

Writing tests

JBuilder provides a wizard for creating new test cases. Select File → New... → Test → Test Case. You can type in the name of the test-case class (see Figure 17).

JBuilder's ErrorInsight combines smoothly with JUnit for test-driven development. Type in a test that refers to classes or methods you have not yet created, and JBuilder will offer to create the missing elements for you (see Figure 18).

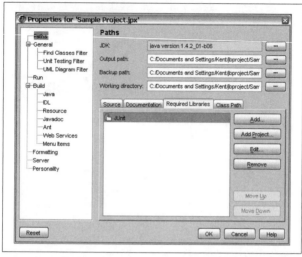

Figure 16. Adding the JUnit Library to an existing project

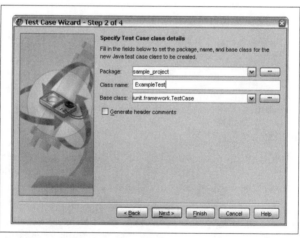

Figure 17. New Test Case Wizard

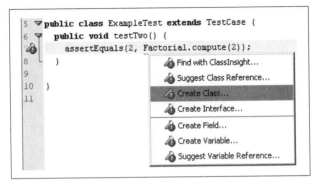

Figure 18. ErrorInsight creates a missing class for you

One of the design decisions we made in JUnit was keeping the testing methods in the same class as the code for creating and deleting test fixtures. This is potentially risky if you want to use the same fixture with test methods in several different classes or the same test methods with several different fixtures. In practice, this isn't usually a problem. You can create an abstract superclass for the common test fixture and put various sets of test methods in the different subclasses. However, this is a pragmatic solution, not necessarily the cleanest design.

JBuilder supports pure fixture classes, classes that create and delete predictable sets of objects. The fixture classes support setUp( ) and tearDown( ) methods that you can override. JBuilder has wizards for fixtures that create JDBC connections, perform JNDI lookups, build own custom fixtures. The test case wizard contains a page to specify which fixtures to create and initialize when an instance of your test class is initialized.

Running tests

JBuilder integrates a convenient test runner with links to the rest of the IDE, as shown in Figure 19.

Figure 19. Test Runner Output

The icons on the left show:

- The hierarchy of tests that were run
- The output of the tests
- The failures and errors

The failures and errors view on the right shows links to source files using the familiar browser link format. For example, clicking on SampleTest.java:8 above navigates to that file and line.

IntelliJ IDEA

IntelliJ IDEA, from JetBrains, has also embraced writing and running JUnit tests as part of the normal flow of programming. The JUnit integration makes it natural to write and run tests, and to code test-first.

Setting up a project so you can write tests

You need to add the JUnit library as a library for your module (a project in IDEA can have several modules.) Select a module in which you want to write tests. Choose File → Module Settings.... Select the Libraries (Classpath) tab in the resulting dialog (Figure 20).

Select Add Jar/Directory.... Navigate to the *JUnit JAR* file. IDEA comes with a version of JUnit, illustrated in Figure 21.

Click OK twice. Now you are ready to start writing tests.

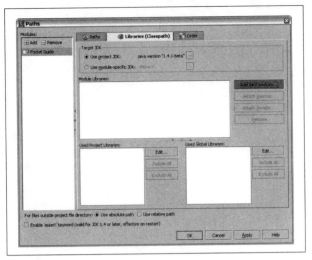

Figure 20. Adding the JUnit JAR

Writing tests

Writing tests in IDEA is just the same as writing any other Java class. There are no special templates or shortcuts. Create a class using the New → Class context menu item on a package. When you edit the generated class code, you will have to extend junit.framework.TestCase. IDEA helps insert the correct import for you, as shown in Figure 22.

Write test methods just as you would write any other Java method. Again, there are no templates or shortcuts to help you, but typing in a new class or method is not that much work. Code completion gives you a handy overview of the variations of the assertXXX methods available, as shown in Figure 23.

Intention Actions in IDEA help when you are coding test-first. They allow you to quickly create classes and methods

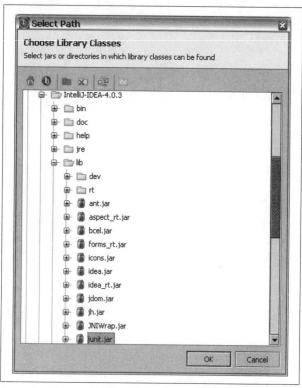

Figure 21. Choosing the JUnit JAR

Figure 22. Automatically inserting the import statement

referred to in your tests. Figure 24 shows IDEA offering to create a missing method.

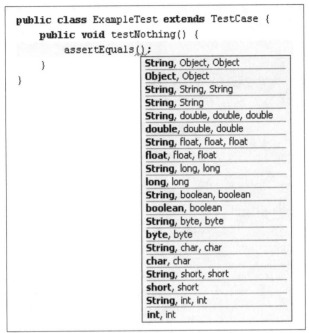

Figure 23. Automatically completing the assertEquals call

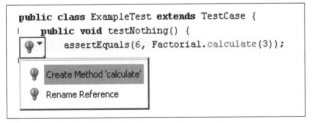

Figure 24. Automatically creating a stub method

Figure 25 shows the stub method IDEA created. IDEA chooses reasonable defaults for types and variables names and offers alternatives.

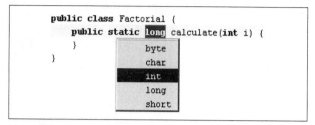

Figure 25. Assistance filling in the correct return type

Running tests

Running any Java program in IDEA is controlled by a "run configuration," a description of all the parameters to be used to run the program. There are several flavors of run configuration. One runs tests and reports the results. Run configurations can be created manually or automatically from the various places in the user interface. This is described later. To create a JUnit run configuration manually, select the menu item Run → Edit Configurations. Press the JUnit tab, and you'll see the dialog shown in Figure 26.

You have three options:

- Run all the tests in a given package
- Run all the tests in a given class
- Run a single test in a given class

IDEA will create a run configuration for you. Figure 27 shows the Run "All Tests" menu item on a package. This item creates a run configuration containing all the tests in the selected package and all dependents and then runs it. When you press the Run button after this, these tests will be rerun.

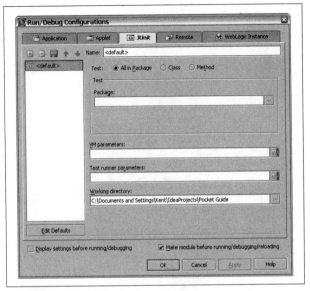

Figure 26. Run configuration for a JUnit test

IDEA will also create and execute a run configuration for you from inside the text editor. If the insertion point is inside the text of a test class, you will see the Run menu item in the context menu, as shown in Figure 28.

The test runner in IDEA has the most features of the IDEs covered here. Figure 29 shows the output of a failed test.

While the tests are running, the controls along the left side allow you to pause, stop the tests, or rerun a single test. The controls along the top allow you to filter the test results and control how selecting test results affects the text editor—for example, scrolling to the source of a selected test.

The Output tab of the right pane of the test runner shows the raw output of the selected test (any text written to the console) and the stack trace of any failure or error. The

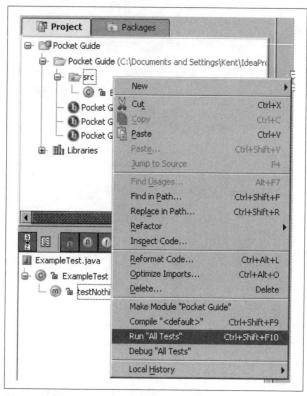

Figure 27. Running the tests

Statistics tab, shown in Figure 30, shows how long each test took, its result, and how much memory it consumed. I find it useful in finding out which tests are slow.

Test Infection

Some programmers have made writing tests part of the daily business of programming. Erich Gamma invented the phrase "test-infected" to describe this habit. When you are test-

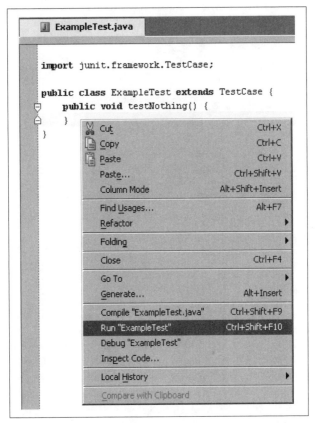

Figure 28. Running a particular test

infected, you habitually see programming problems in terms of tests first and implementation later. When someone describes a problem, the first question you ask yourself is "How would I test for that?" not "What is going on?" The test-infected spend less time debugging and more time designing; less time implementing and more time thinking about what they are doing.

Figure 29. Feedback from a failed test

Test	Time elapsed	Usage Delta	Usage Before	Usage After	Results
Total:	**0.01 s**	**23 kb**	**704 kb**	**432 kb**	**F:1 P:1**
testNothing (Exam	0.01 s	22 kb	704 kb	726 kb	**Assertion**
testNothing2 (Exam	0.0 s	0 kb	432 kb	432 kb	Passed

Figure 30. Tabular feedback from a test run

How do you get infected? First, write lots of tests. Write tests
for obvious problems. Write tests for complicated problems.
If you get stuck on a problem, and you can't think of how to
write a test for it, go back later and write the test once you
have figured it out. Writers write. The test-infected test.

Second, run your tests often. Martin Fowler told one of the
early JUnit stories in which he helped a team write a bunch
of tests and got them all to run. A month later he visited the
same team, which was having serious problems by that time.
They had not run the tests since his last visit. When he ran
the tests, several of them were broken. The tests were written such that if they didn't run, there was no way the system
as a whole could run. If they had just run their tests, they
would have saved the cost of an expensive consultant. (As a
consultant, I have mixed feelings about sharing this advice.)

I instrumented my IDE once as an experiment to see how often I ran some tests. For most of my programming day I was running some tests every minute or two. Longer gaps were attributable to breaks. Sometimes when I'm feeling particularly uncertain, I run tests two or three times just to be sure. Even this frequency of test running isn't outrageous. David Saff and Michael Ernst at MIT invented continuous testing, where tests are run constantly in the background, much as compilers are run in modern IDEs.

Third, learn the design skills necessary to write tests that are simple and run fast. Systems of mostly-independent objects are easier to test. Expensive resources (like connections to a database) can be stubbed out to provide tests that run very quickly. Getting feedback about a system is not just running tests frequently, but writing fast, effective tests so you *can* run them frequently. You can run a thousand tests in a second if you can figure out how to make them each run in a millisecond.

Fourth, once you are infected, start sharing your skills with others. Teaching someone else helps refine your skills. Once two of you are infected, you can reinforce each other's learning.

How many tests you write depends on a balance between ship dates, acceptable quality, work culture, management expectations, and personal need for reassurance and confidence. I test enough to meet my need for clean design and working code I can be proud of.

Teams that track their time carefully report that they spend one-third to one-half of their time writing tests. This time includes design and analysis time as well. Writing tests is an opportunity to make concrete decisions about what you are and are not programming and how you are going to represent the functionality you are implementing. These measurements align with my observations of my own habits well enough for me to trust them as a basic benchmark.

One more hint before I close. If I'm working on a team, and the rest of the team is counting on me to keep my code running, I'm careful to make sure all of our tests run perfectly before committing changes to the shared code. However, if I'm working by myself, I find it helpful to leave the last test broken at the end of the day. When I arrive in the morning, I know just what to do to get started: fix that test. That's usually enough to get me started on my day.

Developer testing is a low-risk way to improve software development. It gives you fewer defects, better designs, higher productivity, and clear communication at little or no cost. You don't need permission or funding to get started. You already have what you need to improve both your software development process and your experience of it. I hope you have fun writing and running tests with JUnit.

Bibliography

Christopher Alexander, *The Timeless Way of Building*, Oxford University Press, 1979. This is the book from which I got the idea of analyzing, designing, testing, and coding programs a little at a time, a process Alexander calls "gradual stiffening." By deferring as many decisions as possible you give yourself as much context as possible to make better decisions when they are unavoidable.

David Astels, *A Practical Guide to Test-Driven Development*. The Jolt-Award winning introduction.

Kent Beck, *Smalltalk Best Practice Patterns*, Prentice-Hall, 1996. Implementation patterns for Smalltalk, many of which apply equally to Java.

Kent Beck, *Extreme Programming Explained: Embrace Change*, Addison-Wesley, 2004. Shows what can be done with developer testing once it has been mastered. The goal is to have positive, mutual relationships between everyone involved in software development.

Kent Beck, *Test-Driven Development*, Addison-Wesley, 2002. A thorough treatment of test-first programming and incremental design. The thorough examples now they seem to me to move kind of slowly, but the section on testing patterns is helpful for learning techniques.

Erich Gamma, Richard Helms, Ralph Johnson, and John Vlissides, *Design Patterns: Elements of Reusable Object-Oriented Software*, Addison-Wesley, 1995. The classic book on designing object-oriented programs.

David Saff and Michael D. Ernst, *An Experimental Evaluation of Continuous Testing During Development*, in ISSTA 2004, Proceedings of the 2004 International Symposium on Software Testing and Analysis (Boston, MA, USA), July 12-14, 2004, pp. 76-85.

Acknowledgments

I would like to thank my reviewers, Erich Gamma, Martin Fowler, and Beth Andres-Beck for their help improving the readability and accuracy of this book. I would like to thank Mike Clark and Erik Meade for maintaining the JUnit FAQ and web site respectively. I would like to thank Erich Gamma for being an outstanding programming partner from the beaches of Sardinia to the top of the Alps. I would like to thank Mike Hendrickson for sponsoring this book at O'Reilly. Finally, I would like to thank Cynthia Andres for editing another book of mine, and for doing such a thorough and patient job.

Index

We'd like to hear your suggestions for improving our indexes. Send email to
index@oreilly.com.

Related Titles Available from O'Reilly

Java

Ant: The Definitive Guide

Better, Faster, Lighter Java

Eclipse

Eclipse Cookbook

Enterprise JavaBeans, *4th Edition*

Hardcore Java

Head First Java

Head First Servlets & JSP

Head First EJB

Hibernate: A Developer's Notebook

J2EE Design Patterns

Java 1.5 Tiger: A Developer's Notebook

Java & XML Data Binding

Java & XML

Java Cookbook, *2nd Edition*

Java Data Objects

Java Database Best Practices

Java Enterprise Best Practices

Java Enterprise in a Nutshell, *2nd Edition*

Java Examples in a Nutshell, *3rd Edition*

Java Extreme Programming Cookbook

Java in a Nutshell, *4th Edition*

Java Management Extensions

Java Message Service

Java Network Programming, *2nd Edition*

Java NIO

Java Performance Tuning, *2nd Edition*

Java RMI

Java Security, *2nd Edition*

JavaServer Faces

Java ServerPages, *2nd Edition*

Java Servlet & JSP Cookbook

Java Servlet Programming, *2nd Edition*

Java Swing, 2nd Edition

Java Web Services in a Nutshell

Learning Java, *2nd Edition*

Mac OS X for Java Geeks

Programming Jakarta Struts *2nd Edition*

Tomcat: The Definitive Guide

WebLogic: The Definitive Guide

O'REILLY®

Our books are available at most retail and online bookstores.
To order direct: 1-800-998-9938 • *order@oreilly.com* • *www.oreilly.com*
Online editions of most O'Reilly titles are available at *safari.oreilly.com*

Keep in touch with O'Reilly

1. Download examples from our books

To find example files for a book, go to:
www.oreilly.com/catalog

select the book, and follow the "Examples" link.

2. Register your O'Reilly books

Register your book at *register.oreilly.com*

Why register your books? Once you've registered your O'Reilly books you can:

- Win O'Reilly books, T-shirts or discount coupons in our monthly drawing.

- Get special offers available only to registered O'Reilly customers.

- Get catalogs announcing new books (US and UK only).

- Get email notification of new editions of the O'Reilly books you own.

3. Join our email lists

Sign up to get topic-specific email announcements of new books and conferences, special offers, and O'Reilly Network technology newsletters at:
elists.oreilly.com

It's easy to customize your free elists subscription so you'll get exactly the O'Reilly news you want.

4. Get the latest news, tips, and tools
www.oreilly.com

- "Top 100 Sites on the Web"—PC Magazine

- CIO Magazine's Web Business 50 Awards

Our web site contains a library of comprehensive product information (including book excerpts and tables of contents), downloadable software, background articles, interviews with technology leaders, links to relevant sites, book cover art, and more.

5. Work for O'Reilly

Check out our web site for current employment opportunities:
jobs.oreilly.com

6. Contact us

O'Reilly & Associates
1005 Gravenstein Hwy North
Sebastopol, CA 95472 USA

TEL: 707-827-7000 or 800-998-9938
(6am to 5pm PST)

FAX: 707-829-0104

order@oreilly.com
> For answers to problems regarding your order or our products.
> To place a book order online, visit:
> *www.oreilly.com/order_new*

catalog@oreilly.com
> To request a copy of our latest catalog.

booktech@oreilly.com
> For book content technical questions or corrections.

corporate@oreilly.com
> For educational, library, government, and corporate sales.

proposals@oreilly.com
> To submit new book proposals to our editors and product managers.

international@oreilly.com
> For information about our international distributors or translation queries. For a list of our distributors outside of North America check out:
> *international.oreilly.com/distributors.html*

adoption@oreilly.com
> For information about academic use of O'Reilly books, visit:
> *academic.oreilly.com*

O'REILLY®

Our books are available at most retail and online bookstores.
To order direct: 1-800-998-9938 • *order@oreilly.com* • *www.oreilly.com*
Online editions of most O'Reilly titles are available at *safari.oreilly.com*